Grant's Aunts from France

Kelly Doudna

Consulting Editor, Diane Craig, M.A./Reading Specialist

Published by ABDO Publishing Company, 4940 Viking Drive, Edina, Minnesota 55435.

Printed in the United States.

Credits
Edited by: Pam Price
Curriculum Coordinator: Nancy Tuminelly
Cover and Interior Design and Production: Mighty Media
Photo and Illustration Credits: BananaStock Ltd., Eyewire Images, Hemera, Image 100, Image Source, PhotoDisc, Stockbyte

Library of Congress Cataloging-in-Publication Data

Doudna, Kelly, 1963-
    Grant's aunts from France / Kelly Doudna.
        p. cm. -- (Rhyme time)
    Includes index.
    ISBN 1-59197-792-4 (hardcover)
    ISBN 1-59197-898-X (paperback)
    1. English language--Rhyme--Juvenile literature. I. Title. II. Rhyme time (ABDO Publishing Company)

PE1517.D68 2004
428.1'3--dc22
                                                                                        2004049515

SandCastle™ books are created by a professional team of educators, reading specialists, and content developers around five essential components that include phonemic awareness, phonics, vocabulary, text comprehension, and fluency. All books are written, reviewed, and leveled for guided reading, early intervention reading, and Accelerated Reader® programs and designed for use in shared, guided, and independent reading and writing activities to support a balanced approach to literacy instruction.

Let Us Know

After reading the book, SandCastle would like you to tell us your stories about reading. What is your favorite page? Was there something hard that you needed help with? Share the ups and downs of learning to read. We want to hear from you! To get posted on the ABDO Publishing Company Web site, send us e-mail at:

sandcastle@abdopub.com

SandCastle Level: Transitional

Words that rhyme do not have to be spelled the same. These words rhyme with each other:

ants

France

aunts

glance

chance

pants

chants

plants

dance

prance

Larry is ahead of the others.

He has a **chance** to score a goal.

Angie is having a picnic with her parents.

She hopes there aren't any **ants**.

Erin likes to **dance** with her umbrella.

Brenda's dad has two sisters.

They are her favorite **aunts**.

Luke and Kyle watch the game.

Luke chants, "Hey batter batter, swing!"

Nick likes to learn about different countries.

Today he is studying **France**.

Sam can read music.

He knows what notes to play after just one **glance**.

Christy's team wears white baseball **pants** and shirts with red sleeves.

Vicky and Isabel have fun on the beach.

They run and prance.

Ella and Terry are potting some plants in the garden.

Grant's Aunts from France

Grant had visitors from France.

His visitors from France
were three of his aunts.

14

Because he didn't know in advance, Grant had no chance to make plans for his aunts.

Grant thought that maybe his aunts could water the plants.

Or maybe his aunts
might go shop for some pants.

Or perhaps Grant's aunts
would find a parade
and watch horses prance.

If they could find a monk,
maybe they could even
learn some chants.

But then by chance
Grant remembered
that his aunts
could dance.

So he spent
the afternoon
in a trance
watching his aunts
from France dance.

Rhyming Riddle

What do you call bugs doing ballet?

Ants dance

Glossary

chant. to say or sing the same words or sounds over and over; a short, simple set of sounds or words sung on just a note or two

glance. a quick look

monk. a man who belongs to a religious group and lives in a monastery

pot. to place in a pot, such as a flowerpot

prance. to walk in a lively, springy way

trance. a state of being completely absorbed in something

About SandCastle™

A professional team of educators, reading specialists, and content developers created the SandCastle™ series to support young readers as they develop reading skills and strategies and increase their general knowledge. The SandCastle™ series has four levels that correspond to early literacy development in young children. The levels are provided to help teachers and parents select the appropriate books for young readers.

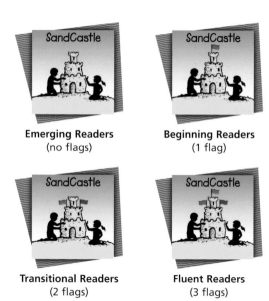

Emerging Readers
(no flags)

Beginning Readers
(1 flag)

Transitional Readers
(2 flags)

Fluent Readers
(3 flags)

These levels are meant only as a guide. All levels are subject to change.

To see a complete list of SandCastle™ books and other nonfiction titles from ABDO Publishing Company, visit www.abdopub.com or contact us at:
4940 Viking Drive, Edina, Minnesota 55435 • 1-800-800-1312 • fax: 1-952-831-1632